ISBN: 978-0692470657 (The Judy Stakee Company & Param Media)

Printed in the United States of America

If you are serious about songwriting you'll find treasures in Judy Stakee's wonderful book. Good creative tools and advice about the craft of writing... as well as solid music business advice from an iconic song plugger. Songwriting 101. Recommended!

— Paul Williams
Songwriter

Judy has written a book that will easily become a staple in the education of a songwriter. She gives sound advice about how important the creative process is to anyone looking to better their craft.

— Jeffrey Rabhan
Chair, Clive Davis Institute of Recorded Music at New York University's Tisch School of the Arts

This book isn't a survival guide. It's an inspiring manual for songwriters and artists who truly want to succeed. Once you start reading it, you won't want to stop!

— Michael Laskow
Founder & CEO, Taxi.com

Dedicated to future storytellers.

The
SONGWRITER'S
SURVIVAL
GUIDE

By Judy Stakee

Table of Contents

FOREWORD
By Sheryl Crow

It is an honor to share with you the gratitude I feel at having met Judy Stakee at the beginning of my journey as a solo artist.

We all need help in achieving our dreams, and Judy showed up at the perfect moment, just when I most needed her, all those years ago. I was fortunate at that time to have back-up gigs with great performers steadily coming my way, but that's not what I ultimately wanted. I felt a powerful urge to break out on my own, to discover who I was really meant to be, both as a performer and as a person. I dreamed of being out in front, sharing my unique point of view and connecting with my fans, and Judy played a pivotal role in helping those dreams become a reality.

In 1989, just after I had finished touring with Michael Jackson, I signed a publishing deal with Judy at

Warner Chappell Music. Working with Judy was an extraordinary experience, one that allowed me the freedom to explore and discover my own voice. She was constantly asking me questions about what I wanted and encouraging me to follow my heart.

We would meet nearly every morning for breakfast at Hugo's on Santa Monica Boulevard, spending hours brainstorming how to create my own pathway in the music industry. My role, first and foremost, was to write, and hers was to be my mirror. I trusted her to critique my songs, and virtually every facet of my budding career, and the two of us quickly formed a winning team. The most important part, of course, was to develop a strong list of songs, after which everything else fell into place.

Judy has spent over two decades helping to build the careers of many incredibly successful performers and writers. In The Songwriter's Survival Guide, she generously shares with you the fundamentals of what it takes to make it in the music business as a songwriter. She also reminds us that while nothing worthwhile is easy - it takes hard work no matter what path you decide to take - it's definitely a lot easier when you have someone knowledgeable on your side, cheering for you and guiding you along the way. I strongly encourage you to listen closely to what she has to say. Her methodology can guide you to success in everything from writing a hit song to learning how to handle meetings with industry executives, while her wealth of stories will inspire you to make your own dreams come true.

— Sheryl Crow

Introduction

Music is the universal language of mankind.
— Henry Wadsworth Longfellow

Hi there. Let me introduce myself: my name is Judy Stakee, and I am a music publisher.

I spent thirty years in the music industry, officially known as a song plugger, guiding songwriters and artists to find and nourish their own voice, develop their style of storytelling, and educate themselves in the business of their career. I now run my own pro-artist development organization—The Judy Stakee Company—where I have created my own methodology within a new paradigm.

I compare the vision of the old paradigm of the music industry to the legend of Camelot, the castle and court led by King Arthur, that showed us a glimpse of what humanity could aspire to. He created the Round

Table for all his knights with the motto "might for right": their power, or might, should be used to do good in the world.

Imagine, if you will, the old model of the music business and industry where the record company serves as the castle with a moat surrounding and protecting it, and with only one drawbridge to enter. It was a privilege when an artist was signed to a company and invited into the Kingdom of Music.

Each company had their own unique style and character, with business models in place that supported the artists so that they could depend upon the system and entrust it with the building of their careers.

This started with the publishing department, followed by A&R (artist and repertoire), production, publicity, marketing, and distribution; all of them waiting for when an artist would need to call on them to execute their specialty. One of the reasons artists signed with any given record company was the feeling of community they got each time they took meetings there. They also entrusted and relied on the music executives of these large companies to lead the way.

Over the years, the business seemed to get bigger than the talent, and executives ended up fighting with artists about who really had control over the artists' careers. Then came the advent of the Internet, connecting everyone and everything, along with an increased accessibility to home studio equipment, which changed the way we did business. The industry as my colleagues and I knew it finally fell apart in 2005, with the result that it was now easier for the artist to take control of their own career — which is great news for you!

We now live in a world where the music business and the music industry are two separate entities. I compare this new music business to a sort of spaceship, like the Enterprise from *Star Trek*. The ship is run with such precision that when a song is fed into it, the mechanism of the ship can swing into action and promote, brand, market, sell, distribute, and collect royalties, all with a touch of a button.

In this way, the music business does not need to be as involved in the creative process of developing the songwriter and artist anymore. Instead, it can use its creative power in leading and running the machine that turns the art into a sustainable business.

Now the music business is up there in the sky as the Enterprise, fulfilling its role of turning creativity into a profitable business, traveling through the wide universe of time and space. This vast universe is what you—and every songwriter and artist out there waiting to be discovered—has at your disposal to explore when creating your product.

You are now the music industry. You are here to create what you dream of and empower yourself so that you can have the career you want, no matter what obstacles you face along the way. And my role as a music publisher is to help you navigate and build a strong foundation in the music business of today.

While there were parts of the old music business that had to go and would not have survived the digital age, other parts remain relevant today. Most importantly, I feel we have somehow lost the wisdom of that time. It is the ideal of Camelot that I want to resurrect, and properly adapt it to help shape a new paradigm, one where nobility and honor will guide our actions.

One of the ways I am transitioning from the old Camelot ideal to the new Enterprise model is to get rid of the word "perfect" when talking about ourselves and our music. I tried most of my life to be perfect and, not surprisingly, failed. I am done with that now and have a new mantra in my life thanks to a comedy class I took: "There is no such thing as a mistake". This mantra is not meant to be taken literally, of course, as we all make mistakes, but the meaning or intention behind it is very freeing.

The teacher of this comedy class explained to us that your acting partner is a gift, that whatever comes out of their mouth is an opportunity. If your partner 'goofs up' and says something out of the ordinary, that's a million-dollar opportunity for you to shine and create something really unique. It's what we do after we make the mistakes—what we choose to create out of the mistakes—that we need to focus on.

The creative process — the time, space, and tools we put in place so that we can develop — has to be forgiving, allowing the room for us to experiment and create without any harsh judgment. We still need to strive to achieve our ideal so far as we are able, so long as we remain open and forgiving of our inevitable mistakes. The outcome is that we become a more forgiving community filled with compassion for the creative process. My primary goal here is to help you build such a community for yourself.

To get to this new paradigm, I have developed a unique methodology and language for how to write a song and how to develop your craft that will help you navigate this new world of rapidly expanding options and virtually endless possibilities. I have developed a set of practices that, when put into place, will guide you to construct a song, to become knowledgeable on how to build your own career, and to be able to develop yourself in the areas in which you want to grow.

I wrote this book to answer two simple questions:

1) What does it take to become a songwriter?
2) How do I become marketable to a music publisher?

Within these pages, you will find the necessary tools, resources, and inspiration to build a career as a songwriter and help you to attract a music publisher, the person or company who will become a partner in your business.

What is a songwriter?

You can write songs for other artists to perform, and you can also write songs for you or your own musical group to perform, but when I use the term songwriter in this book, I am referring to an individual who only writes songs for other artists.

When I say artist, I am referring to an individual who may write songs for others to record, but also writes and records their own songs.

What does a music publisher do?

A music publisher is the songwriter's partner, and is the

one who takes care of the business and helps guide the songwriter in their craft, so that they can fully concentrate on creating.

As soon as you finish writing a song, you own it as the creator (the author) and as the publisher (the administrator) of that song. Most songwriters are willing to share a piece of their publishing royalties with a music publisher, in exchange for the music publisher taking care of them and their administrative functions related to their songs.

There's a reason why songwriters often refer to their songs as their "babies." As the writer, you create the child, and as the publisher, you take care of that child. Most songwriters can use some extra help with the development and business (a.k.a. "care-taking") aspect of their careers; therefore, the goal is to sign with a music publisher whose main objective is to guide songwriters and take care of their business as it grows. This partnership allows both parties to thrive.

A music publisher provides three main services:

Creative

Music publishers are there to help guide and develop you as a songwriter. They promote and market you and your catalogue of songs for commercial release by getting cuts with other artists, obtaining licensing placements in film and TV, helping secure record deals, and even financing recordings.

One of their main responsibilities is to "pitch" your songs, which means to play a song for an artist or someone who is connected to that artist in the hopes of getting a "cut", to record and release the song commercially. The individual who pitches the songs is called a song plugger, and they will find and generate projects that will showcase your songs from among their network of record executives, producers, and managers.

The technical term for this process is "exploiting", which, in this context, is used in a positive way to express how a music publisher will pitch your songs to the fullest extent possible.

Administration

A music publisher registers and protects your created songs. See *Chapter 6* for more on this topic.

Collection

A music publisher collects the royalties earned from your songs. These royalties come from sales of recordings (from Internet downloads and CD's, as well as songs featured in ringtones, computer games, etc.), songs performed publicly on the radio, and sync and master licenses for all media. (See *Chapter 9* for more on sync and master licenses.) For their total services, they take a percentage from what they collect.

How did I become a music publisher? This is my story.

My mother says I came out of the womb singing and dancing. As her due date approached, she awoke at midnight after a dinner of Mexican food, not with heartburn, but with me demanding to make my entrance into the world. I was born barely two hours later, deliberate in my entrance and already sure of my voice. From that moment on, I was a child who constantly made noise, dancing and singing all the time.

I became aware at a very early age of the fact that music had the power to move and heal the soul. Music is what saved me. I did not grow up having the kind of dialogue with my parents that I would have wished, so I turned instead to the lyrics of songs to guide me. When I started to tackle issues like my relationship with my parents, the importance of school for my future, and how to cultivate friendships and other relationships, songs fed me advice.

Growing up in the sixties, the film *The Wizard of Oz* was shown once a year on television. There was no way to record it in case you missed it, and it was likely that you had to watch the whole thing in black and white. It was a big event in our household. Eventually, a record was released that featured not only the soundtrack of the film, but all of the dialogue as well. I couldn't believe it: I could listen to the whole movie over and over, anytime I wanted! Soon enough, I had it memorized in its entirety.

I embraced and lived Dorothy's lessons through her words and songs, and came to identify deeply with the theme that sometimes you have to leave home in order to truly appreciate it. Dorothy learned the importance of independence within the family unit, found her courage by standing up and confronting challenges, and broke her heart wide open to fully understand the importance of love.

I felt like Dorothy's story mirrored my own. Her

signature song, "Somewhere Over the Rainbow", was my anthem. I sang it countless times, until it inhabited every cell in my body. Those words that I believed down to my core became a guide for my own life, and informed my lifelong appreciation for the magic of music.

Navigating any kind of childhood is challenging, but when music is involved, the road is not as rough. Music can comfort us when we are in the growing stages of finding out who we are. The truth is, music has the ability to heal our soul and is there to help us process what we are feeling.

One day when I was six years old, I came home from a friend's house and could talk about nothing but their piano. I was obsessed. That Christmas, my father surprised my sister and me with an upright. (Though the gift was technically for both of us, I secretly claimed it as my own.) My father made a deal with us: we could keep the piano and he would pay for music lessons, and in return we would practice for half an hour a day on weekdays and fifteen minutes on Saturdays (Sunday would be our day off). The contract he had us sign was to last four years, and after that we could sit down and renegotiate the terms. He wanted us to grow into the ability to really use this wonderful instrument to make music, to entertain ourselves and others. I ended up taking lessons for thirteen years. At that young age, I was already in business thanks to this contract with my father.

My music lessons encompassed not only piano, but also voice. I couldn't be happier: I thought making music, whatever form it took, was the coolest thing on earth. From then on, I never wanted anything else but to make a life with music in it, no matter what. So I studied, practiced, and worked hard, eventually receiving a voice and academic scholarship to the University of Southern California in Los Angeles, California.

During those four years, though I learned more theory, composition, and orchestral knowledge than I could ever recall, I did get the opportunity to sing every day. Besides that, I was the musical director of my sorority house, putting on shows and leading songfests. And in my last two years of college, I worked at a dinner theater club four nights a week, where we performed short versions of Broadway musicals and original numbers. For the price of dinner, the audience was entertained by kids like me, who just loved to sing! During this time, I also took dance classes and got as much acting experience as I could under my belt.

In June of 1978, I graduated with my music degree, and was immediately faced with some big questions: What am I going to do now? How am I going to turn my passion into a career? How am I going to support myself? My sorority sisters were all signing up for entry-level sales jobs at IBM, and I could not think of a worse path for me to follow. I began to panic as I tried to find a job that would suit me, when I met a woman who had moved to LA to work in the music business. All I could think was, "Where do I sign up?!" I followed her down the yellow brick road and entered the music industry, which I would come to call home for the rest of my life.

The music industry at that time was a community focused on identifying, developing, recording, and releasing artists to the world. The song was the seed for all of it. My first publishing job was for Arista Music, the publishing division of Arista Records run by Clive Davis.

Aside from guiding and protecting songwriters, I had access to amazing artists to pitch songs to and was introduced to artists who also wrote their own songs. My first big cut was with Barry Manilow, a song called "Some Girls" by Mike Chapman and Nicky Chinn off Manilow's *Here Comes The Night* album.

I quickly learned that the first stop on the path of an artist is at the music publisher's door, and I had positioned myself where it all begins. If artists needed a song to sing because they didn't write their own, or if they needed to work on their songs to make them good enough for their next album, that's where I, as the music publisher, came in. I got to help songwriters at the very beginning of their career, assessing their situation and helping them to not waste their time and money demoing songs before they were truly ready.

What I soon discovered was that my gift lay in bringing to light the unique talent of each individual songwriter and artist. I have the ability to act as a mirror, one that has a vault behind it filled with inspiration, education, homework, and success stories that enable me to reflect back a clear image. This then allows the songwriter or artist to consciously choose what they want and need and how to achieve it. I have been developing this gift from the very beginning of my career as a song plugger: just imagine what my vault looks like today with over thirty years of experience in it!

I became known throughout my career as the 'champion of the songwriter', and I wrote this book in order to provide you, the songwriter, with the tools that you will need to forge your career. What you do with that career is up to you: the possibilities are virtually endless.

You can write songs for other people, pen commercial jingles, write for the Broadway stage, teach others how to write songs, become a spoken word artist, or simply write songs for yourself and your loved ones. You can also share your songs through online mediums such as YouTube, which can be an end unto itself, as it's a way to grow a fan base and earn revenue through ads, touring, etc.—or it can lead to other career opportunities (i.e. getting signed to a label).

Regardless of your particular career goals, I will help you put in place a creative process that will allow you to develop your writing and musical skills by challenging your body, mind, and soul. Indeed, this book will not only teach you the ins and outs of navigating the music industry, but through my methodology, personal stories, and practical advice, you will also learn how to put a foundation in place to support you in reaching your full potential as a songwriter.

Songwriters are the foundation of the music business. Without their creative output, the music business would never survive. It simply would not exist.

1

MY METHODOLOGY
Developing Yourself

We shall not cease from exploration and the end of
all our exploring will be to arrive where we started
and know the place for the first time.
— T.S. Eliot

There are no two people in this world who are exactly
alike. However, we all need similar guidance in creating our
lives; we all need encouragement, education in our chosen
field, an understanding of the rules of the game, and a
strategy for how to reach our goals.

How you process that guidance and integrate it
with who you are as a human being is ultimately what
guides you to your full potential. It's amazing how having
the right knowledge can be so freeing. I still feel such joy
when I see a songwriter's face light up after receiving a tool

or a piece of information that leads them to their transformation.

The music business that I grew up in provided a safe container for the creative process. All the time, space, and tools required to develop artists and songwriters were there. (See *Chapter 2* for more on these tools.) But times have changed. Now, it's up to each individual to take on that responsibility and prove that they can handle their own careers. In the long run, this shift benefits the artist and songwriter, allowing them to have flexibility in their goals as they develop.

So, how do you get better and move ahead in this industry? That's the million-dollar question, isn't it? You get better by evolving. Your ability to develop is directly related to what you will achieve. The better you become at evolving, the better your results will be.

I have worked with many artists over the years, and what I found to be missing most often was a common language that both parties could use to communicate. To address these communication issues, I have created an easily understandable methodology that puts in place a framework to help artists and songwriters to develop themselves. This methodology is based on two very simple but powerful questions. The first question is: What is a song? And the second is: How do you develop yourself so that you can write more effective songs?

What is a song?

A song is the integration of voice, lyrics, and melody. It is the product that you are going to create.

The voice that sings the song has the power to make that song tangible. I never exclude the voice when I am speaking about or critiquing a song. It is just as important as the melody and lyrics (if not sometimes more so).

Lyrics are the words you put together in a certain order so that you can tell your story. There are so many to choose from. Which ones resonate most deeply with you? The melody represents your emotions and feelings. After the basics (happiness, excitement, tenderness, fear, anger, sadness), a nearly endless supply opens up to you when you start pairing them up, and they become another emotion completely. For example, put anticipation and joy together and you get optimism. (We will explore the primary emotions and their combinations more in *Chapter 3*.)

How do you develop yourself?

We experience life in three ways: through body, mind, and soul. This encompasses anything we can touch, know, or feel.

> *Body:* your structure
> *Mind:* your intellect
> *Soul:* your essence

You will have to develop facets of your body, mind, and soul in order to achieve results in your voice, lyrics, and melody and effectively create songs. In other words, you will need to be inspired, nurtured, and educated in all of these areas in order for you to succeed as a songwriter.

Let's take it a step further. The following six tools will help lay the foundation from which you will build your creative process, both for writing your songs and for developing yourself as a songwriter.

1. Your body is your container. Your voice does not exist without your body. How do you keep your body in shape?

2. Your voice is your power to communicate. How are you taking care of your voice?

3. Your mind is made up of the collective aspects of consciousness and thought. How do you keep your mind in shape?

4. The lyrics are your words arranged to tell your perspective on life. What is your style of storytelling?

5. Your soul is you and all that you are. Are you listening to yourself and giving yourself what you need?

6. The melodies are your emotions expressed through sound. Are you paying attention to all of your feelings?

Let's take a look at an example. If you wanted to run a marathon, then you would be put through a rigorous training program that would include your body (eating healthier and running long distances every day), your mind (studying past races, techniques, and strategies for your game plan to win), and your soul (growing spiritually and psychologically in order to be able to handle the stress and emotions associated with winning and losing). The same principles apply if you want to become a songwriter.

I believe that the key to developing your voice, melodies, and lyrics is to first incorporate processes into your life with the intention of developing your body, mind, and soul. I have found that by teaching someone to be more aware of the words they choose when they speak, the emotions they carry with them into a room, and the tone of voice they use to steer the conversation, this will determine whether their message is heard, whether they are on or off the stage.

I suggest putting together a process (a series of actions that you take in order to achieve a particular goal) that will help you keep your voice in shape, increase your vocabulary, and inspire you to know who you really are. To help you to do this, I am providing a few suggestions here for developing your body, mind, and soul.

If you want to see fast results, changing something in your body first can help your mind and soul to follow suit. For example, if you do a handstand in the middle of the room for the first time, whether it's on your own or with someone there to spot you, your body will feel a rush of confidence from doing something you may have never thought you could do before. When you stand right side up again, you'll probably be thinking, "Wow, I never thought I could do that! If I can do that, I wonder what else I can do?" Your soul will feel lighter, like it's been stirred and shaken up.

When it comes to your mind, it's essential to adopt a beginner's mindset. Every time you start the process of writing a new song, recording a new album, or building a new tour, I suggest you mentally put yourself right at the beginning, as if it's the first time you ever wrote, sang, or performed. That beginner's mindset asks you to put aside any expectations you may be holding onto so that you can explore more freely.

Can you imagine never learning anything new after leaving school? Even if you got a job and learned how to do it well, you would essentially be stuck in the same place forever.

Be an inquisitive student in the art of songwriting and building your career. Ask yourself: What do I have to learn to be the best? Take on that responsibility and challenge yourself to become your best self.

True story: I met Joy Williams in 2005 after she had released her third and final Christian album. She did not want to remain on that path musically, but did not yet have a vision for who she was without the community of Christian worship music surrounding her. She actually said at the time that she only wanted to write and wasn't sure she would sign another artist deal. But I had no doubt she would sing again.

I spent two years being the mirror she needed in order to heal, nurture, and inspire her body, mind, and soul. I pushed her outside of her comfort zone to experience the challenges she needed in order to grow and to know that she was in charge of creating her vision.

Today, Joy is able to sustain not only a successful solo career, but her music is also licensed consistently in film, TV shows, and commercials. On top of that, she also developed a strong enough voice and chemistry with a partner to create an entirely separate project, *The Civil Wars*, who won four Grammy Awards together! They created a sound that felt like two voices dancing together while they were singing.

And if all that's not enough, her latest solo effort (released in 2015) is yet another conscious move on her part, the latest step in her evolution as a songwriter and artist.

Judy's Must-Read: *You Can Heal Your Life* by Louise Hay. Louise believes, as I do, that the thoughts we think and the words we speak are crucial in shaping our lived experiences.

Challenge yourself with some soul-searching questions on the following page.

What is your creative process?

_____

_____

_____

_____

_____

_____

What is your definition of the word "commitment"?

_____

_____

_____

_____

_____

_____

What emotional state do you often find yourself occupying?

_____

_____

_____

_____

_____

_____

What's stopping you from reaching your goals, from taking a leap of faith, or standing up for yourself?

_____

_____

_____

_____

_____

_____

What do you value most in your life?

_____

_____

_____

_____

_____

_____

_____

What are your greatest talents?

_____

_____

_____

_____

_____

_____

_____

What makes you feel complete and whole?

_____

_____

_____

_____

_____

_____

What do you believe in and stand for?

_____

_____

_____

_____

_____

_____

2

THE CREATIVE PROCESS
Your Room to Grow

There are really three parts to the creative process.
First there is inspiration, then there is the
execution, and finally there is the release.
— Eddie Van Halen

The task at hand is to now build a creative process tailored to your needs, allowing you to take the steps that will enable you to achieve your goals. Whenever I decide to explore a new endeavor, I know I will need the time, space, and tools in order to achieve whatever that might be, whether it's a song, a workshop, or even a vacation plan!
Let's say you wanted to make cakes for a living. No matter how many different types of cakes you bake, from the fanciest to the simplest, you will always need the same basic ingredients, as well as the space itself (a kitchen), the

time (about an hour and a half) and the tools (a bowl, a spoon, measuring cups, an oven, flour, etc.).

It is the same for writing songs.

Imagine building an extra room onto your house for the sole purpose of holding the tools — body/voice, mind/lyrics, and soul/melody — that you need to write your songs. Picture a grand piano in one corner, a yoga mat in another, and on the other side of the room a shelf full of books and a wall full of art that inspires you. All you need now is to find the time to devote yourself to your craft, and you are ready to enter the creative process.

One example of a tool that I advise songwriters to put into this imaginary room is voice lessons. From there, you can start implementing all the other tools in a way that supports what you are trying to achieve. Two more examples would be vocal warm-ups performed each morning and drinking hot lemon tea before a performance. I would suggest that you consciously put these tools in place to guide, nurture, and protect your biggest commodity: yourself.

Finding the time to develop your creative process can be a big challenge, especially when you also have to work or go to school as well. I find that scheduling time in my calendar to work on my craft helps to at least keep my creative process in my consciousness. I have a standing appointment every week with my musical director, who accompanies me on the piano while coaching me through the songs I am preparing for a one-woman showcase that I have been putting together. Some weeks I have to cancel the session, but it's on the books no matter what.

How much time will you allot to one song, to your overall development, to taking care of business? Do you have a weekly writing appointment? Are you taking any music classes? What about devoting two hours a week to just taking care of the business aspects of being a songwriter?

When you can create with intention — which means you have a plan or goal in place that guides your actions — and you are conscious of your thoughts and the words you use to express yourself, your ability to manifest your goals gets a lot better!

The difference between answering the question "What is your goal?" with "I don't know" and "I'm going to win a Grammy one day" is that the second answer will help you to achieve success a whole lot sooner than the first one.

True story: Songwriter, musician, and artist Dillon O'Brian is a genuine storyteller who weaves his personal revelations into songs from a perspective of questioning, wonder, and idealism.

Dillon was a child prodigy on the piano and knew very early on that music was his path in life. After finishing college, Dillon moved to Los Angeles to start his career as a songwriter. Through a UCLA extension course, he met and hired a lyric tutor who helped him to more effectively recognize and express his point of view in his writing. His tutor at UCLA helped Dillon to understand a song from multiple perspectives, from the importance of a title, to what had to be achieved in the first line of a song and how to make a listener really care about a song. Being proactive and taking his career into his own hands has certainly paid off for Dillon.

Dillon was one of my most productive writers, and during the decade we worked together, he wrote and got cuts with everyone from Bonnie Raitt to Shakira, Amy Grant, Vince Gill, and the Celtic Tenors.

Judy's Must-Read: *Toning: The Creative and Healing Power of the Voice* by Laurel Elizabeth Keyes will get you into the perfect mindset to sing.

What do you need in order to build your own creative process? What tools are required to put your ideas into action?

1. What do you do for your body?

What can you do to help develop and care for your body every day? Every week? What about taking a dance class or practicing yoga? What can you put in place on a regular basis that will afford you the time you need to check in with your body?

2. How do you take care of your voice?

Your voice is the tool you use to express who you are. Is yours working to the best of its ability, or is it being stifled? (See *Chapters 3* and *10* for more information on this important topic.)

3. How do you improve your storytelling?

Do you keep a journal? How do you keep track of new vocabulary? A good journal exercise is to write one page every day, taking special care to note any significant events in your life and how they made you feel.

4. How will you hone your craft?

Are you taking classes and workshops in your field of interest? Are you learning a musical instrument? It's never too late, as long as you have the passion.

5. What about acting, musical theater, voice-over and/ or comedy classes?

These all deal with voice, music, and lyrics, but from within different modalities. The flexibility to move between each of these areas can help you to develop a stronger voice within.

6. Do you know how to produce a simple demo of songs?

It will save you a lot of time and energy down the line if you know how to communicate your vision from the start. (See *Chapter 5* for an explanation of how to record your own demo.)

3

IT STARTS WITH A SONG
Building Your Catalogue

*Storytelling reveals meaning without committing the
error of defining it.*

— Hannah Arendt

There are many types of songs, but since songwriters
typically write for other artists, they are working with a
fairly specific definition. It should be noted that when I
talk about songs in this book, I am referring mainly to
popular songs that are played on the radio.

A song is the integration of your voice, your story
told in lyric form, and a melody filled with emotions
realized through the tonal color of pitch and rhythm. It is
an approximately four-minute, two hundred-word
experience that can transform a listener's mood or their
perception of the world.

Songs can be solely written by you, or they can be cowritten. That part is up to you. Either way, you are going to have to generate a catalogue of songs to get started. It would be no different than if you had wanted to be a shoemaker; you would need to make a lot of shoes before creating a pair worthy of showing to a department store. Your songs are your product, and you should take pride in them.

To write a song, you will need your tools of voice, lyrics, and melodies.

Voice.

Your voice will lift the words from the page and allow them to float through the melody. It can be your greatest gift and one of your most powerful tools in expressing yourself.

Your voice does not exist without your body, and it is the sound your body makes when you feel. For example, when my stomach rumbles, my mind identifies the feeling and my voice says out loud, "I'm hungry". Your voice is a pathway of communication between your body and your mind, and between yourself and the world. Recognizing how you feel helps you to identify it with the right words, so that your voice can be clearly understood by yourself and others. It is a unique expression of who you are.

I should tell you now that I think everyone should be singing, no matter who you are or what you do in life. When you sing, your body creates vocalizations and vibrational patterns that can have the power to heal the body on a cellular level, and it's something we don't take nearly as much advantage of as we could. I believe that sound will be part of the next frontier of healing and wellness.

I stopped singing when I began my career, and in my late thirties I developed a thyroid disease — Graves' disease — which affects the hormones and metabolism and is located in the throat. I was forced to take treatments that ruined my vocal chords and left me with no singing voice at all.

Dealing with this illness set me on a lifelong path of finding out how I could heal my own body. Most importantly, I had to ask myself: How do I get my voice back? Looking back now, I meant that literally as well as figuratively, as I had lost my voice in the soulless corporate world that the music industry had become. How could my life move forward if there was no voice to lead it?

What ultimately restored my voice was vocal toning, the sustaining of a single note with the breath. I had a thirty-minute commute to the office and would tone my voice every day in the car, twice a day. I could make the ugliest sounds and no one was there to hear (or, more importantly, judge me!). For close to two years I worked to get my voice back. The amazing thing is that when I started to really sing again, that's when my body truly started to react in a positive way and heal. I really started to understand how the vibrational pattern of singing was healing me both physically and emotionally. Through this healing process, it became perfectly clear to me how important our voice is to all parts of our being.

If you dream of becoming a vocal artist in addition to being a songwriter, then I'm assuming you can already carry a tune; however, just because you can sing, that doesn't mean you don't need to keep developing and honing your vocal chops.

If your plan is to write for other artists and you don't want to be on stage yourself, I know that the task of working on your voice may not be a priority in your mind. However, I still strongly suggest that you sing your own songs for your demos. I think it is always helpful to hear the original rendition of a song in the author's voice, how the author intended it to be heard. You can always hire someone else to sing your songs for a professional demo, but in my experience, the version of a song recorded by the person who wrote it often sells better to the artist than the "produced" version.

Lyrics.

Lyrics are your story, told in your own unique voice. These words tell the story of your perspective on yourself, others, and the world around you. This is your chance to tell your side of the story! For example, "love" is a subject, while "love stinks" is one possible perspective on that subject. You get approximately four minutes and between two hundred and three hundred words to impart this story.

Lyrics can take different structural forms, and I have included a few examples at the end of this chapter. As for how you arrange the words you choose, that is a puzzle for each individual songwriter to figure out. For example, if you use the word "sofa" at the end of a line in your song, you are ending on a vowel, giving the singer the choice of holding the sound for longer. However, if you use the word "couch", there's nowhere to go because you're ending on a consonant, and you have to end the phrase there.

I recommend you start a journal where you can record new words, thoughts, and ideas you come across and try them out to see which ones resonate with you.

Melody.

Melodies are your soul's reflection in sound.

If you play an instrument, then you already have the tools you need to find the notes and chords that correctly express the heartbeat of your story. If you don't play an instrument, I suggest humming your melody into a recorder and then hiring someone to build a track around it. This may also be a good time to find a musician who can cowrite a song with you. (We will explore cowriting in greater depth in *Chapter 4*.) When you put these three components together, a song is born. You have written a short scene set to music and used your voice to communicate the experience to others.

To get better at this process, you will need the next six months to a year of practicing writing over and over. Once you've performed this task enough times, your own unique perspective and style will begin to emerge.

To further your music education, there are many choices you can make on your path. Look into schools like the Berklee School of Music in Boston, Belmont University in Nashville, the Musicians Institute in Los Angeles, the Los Angeles Songwriting School, or Full Sail University in Florida. I would also encourage you to check out workshops, tutors, and online classes; whatever it takes for you to become the songwriter you want to be—or, for that matter, to learn any other skill you want to add to your toolbox.

At this stage of building your career, think of yourself as an entrepreneur who needs to generate a plan of action. This is essential if you want to stay ahead of what is simply popular or trendy in the music world. If you only focus on trying to duplicate what is already out there, by the time your product is ready for the public, you will likely find that it has gone out of style, or is a copy of what already exists on the market.

I built my reputation on knowing how to recognize the potential of something genuinely new. Sheryl Crow was my first!

True story: Nine-time Grammy Award-winner Sheryl Crow is one of the few artists to successfully transition from backup singer to star.

When I met Sheryl in 1988, she was in the middle of her coveted gig singing backup for Michael Jackson's year-long *Bad* tour. She was smart, beautiful, played almost every instrument, had perfect pitch, and embodied a unique perspective on life that shone through in her songwriting. I immediately knew that I wanted to work with her, but she had at least another six months left on the tour. We knew it wasn't possible to begin concentrating on her own career until she was finished her tour with Michael. I would have to wait.

In the meantime, Sheryl did not waste her down time on the road. She had a rig made that was essentially a studio container on wheels measuring five feet high and four feet across. When she unlocked it, all the tools she needed to write and record a demo were there waiting for her: she was a one-person band. She wrote by herself and with her other band mates, including Michael's musical director.

When the tour ended, I listened to a few of her original songs and was blown away. I signed her to a development deal at Warner Chappell Music (an established Music Publishing company), further encouraging her to develop her own voice, both on and off stage.

That first year after signing her deal, Sheryl and I spent days on end concentrating on and discovering what melodies and stories she could create that would tell the world her point of view. I became the best mirror I could be for Sheryl. She tried out every outfit, idea, whim, lyric, and melody on me, and I offered her my reflective views and guidance.

We were, from the very beginning, both the student and the teacher. As much as I taught her about writing and artistry, she taught me how to guide a devoted and disciplined student. For example, she fed on my critiquing her songs so that she could turn them into hits. She did not take my critiques personally, but trusted that I only wanted the best for her. That attitude propelled the process of her development forward. She listened to what I had to say, executed my advice, and really set the bar for my future clients in terms of self-discipline.

I helped Sheryl build a catalogue of songs that allowed us to introduce her to the community of musicians, writers, and executives she wanted to belong to. And those first songs landed her a record contract, manager, producer, agent, lawyer, and business manager!

Remember: songs are your calling card. Always.

Judy's Must-Read: *From the Horse's Mouth: Oxford Dictionary of English Idioms* is a wonderful source of lyrical inspiration.

Ideas to Start a Song:

Hit a wall? Stuck in a rut? Got a bad case of writer's block? Use these ten questions as a starting point to give your mind a nudge forward.

1. If you could have any artist cut one of your songs, who would you write a song for?

Example:

If you pick Carrie Underwood, you'll want to write something that you know she would want to sing about. Pay attention to the word choices she uses in her songs; she sings about female empowerment told through very visual stories. And keep in mind her wide vocal range when you're writing the melodies.

If you pick One Direction, you will be writing melodies with harmonies and lyrically telling stories from a younger male perspective. Read through their lyrics to find out how they convey their message.

2. Pick a theme from the list below. Write a one-page journal entry on your perspective on each one.

Examples:
Power of words
Loss of love
Quest for self-discovery
Isolation
Loss of innocence
Rebirth
Fear of failure
Progress – real or illusion
Everlasting love

3. Write a 10- to 15-second musical motif that will set the whole mood for your song before a word is uttered.

Songs with great intros are wonderful for film and TV placements. Imagine the scene you are writing for and the perfect imagery to accompany it.

Personally, I love how The Fray's "How To Save A Life" starts with a seven-second piano interlude that immediately sets the tone for the whole song. The song was first featured on ABC's Grey's Anatomy during its second season and then became an "unofficial theme" on the show, leading to it being used in the main promotions for the show's third season.

4. What was the last great movie you saw? Write a song about your favorite scene.

How is your perspective on this scene unique? Describe what you saw and how it made you feel, sparing no detail.

5. Choose a musical genre.

Country, pop, rock, urban, electronic, adult contemporary, Christian… the possibilities are varied and nearly endless.

Pick one for this exercise and embrace it. For an extra challenge, go with a genre that falls outside of your comfort zone. If you've had experience writing pop songs aimed at a younger demographic, try taking on country or urban.

6. Ask a friend to give you an opening line about any topic, and write a song from there.

Build a story from that one sentence of inspiration.
Example: "I was looking through some photographs..."

7. Stop and take a look around you. Write about an object that you see close at hand.

Take a cue from Jason Mraz, who wrote an entire song about his coffee cup.

8. Pick an emotion to write from.

What are you feeling right this moment? Pin down the emotion you're feeling, then use it. Have you heard of the eight primary emotions, grouped on a positive or negative basis? Joy versus sadness; anger versus fear; trust versus distrust; surprise versus anticipation. Similarly to the way primary colors combine, primary emotions can blend together to form the full spectrum of the human emotional experience. For example, sadness and disgust can blend to form remorse.

9. Tell a recent story.

Has anything significant or life-changing happened to you recently? Write a journal entry about this event to figure out what angle you can take.

10. Throw caution to the wind.

Close your eyes and just start singing. See what comes out with no expectations whatsoever. You may surprise yourself!

I hope your mind is whirling with ideas and inspiration for your next song. Jot them down on the next few pages before we move on.

_____

_____

_____

_____

_____

_____

_____

_____

_____

_____

_____

_____

_____

_____

_____

_____

_____

_____

_____

_____

_____

_____

_____

_____

_____

_____

_____

_____

_____

_____

_____

_____

_____

_____

_____

_____

_____

_____

_____

_____

_____

_____

_____

Lyrical Structures

Example 1

A	Verse
A	Verse (optional)
B	Chorus
A	Verse
B	Chorus
C	Bridge
B	Chorus

Example 2

A	Verse
	Pre-Chorus
B	Chorus
A	Verse
	Pre-Chorus
B	Chorus
C	Bridge
B	Chorus

Example 3

A	Verse
	Chorus at the end of each verse
A	Verse
	Chorus at the end of each verse
B	Bridge
A	Verse
	Chorus at the end of each verse

4

COWRITING
Playing Well with Others

Politeness is the poison of collaboration.
— Edwin Land

Cowriting is when two or more songwriters collaborate to create a song.

I can hear melodies in my head and love writing lyrics, but it's been a few years since I've played piano, so I like to collaborate with musicians to bring songs to life. I am always in awe of the writers who can do it all by themselves. If you do need someone to help you out, however, then I suggest finding a cowriter.

In my years of experience in the music industry, I have come across many writers who would benefit from collaborating, but who strongly resisted it. Fear, pride, selfishness, and distrust are all obstacles that stand in the way of a writer being willing to cowrite.

However, I strongly believe that collaboration can be crucial to your career. Think of it as an investment strategy that will help propel you towards accomplishing your dreams. Cowriting helps shed light on exactly where you are in the development of your craft.

Everything we are about in this life is in relation to someone or something else. For example, I am small compared to a building and huge compared to a flower; where you are weak, someone else is strong. If you are talented at writing lyrics and melodies, you can benefit from a partner who is an excellent producer or multi-instrumentalist with a working knowledge of music theory and chord structures. You both win and help each other at the same time.

Building relationships (whether it's through cowriting a song or otherwise) directly builds your network. As a songwriter, you want to have a network of people in place who know who you are (your character) and what you do (your skills). This network of people can open up opportunities you never would have come across otherwise. For instance, your cowriter may know someone whose friend or relative is a record executive at a big music label. You never know what possibilities are waiting for you!

One of my favorite quotes is this African proverb: "It takes a village to raise a child". I don't know anyone who can achieve greatness all on their own. We all need others to help guide, educate, and inspire us.

Here's some advice for your next cowriting project:

Be intentional.

You are always faced with a choice when you find yourself in the room with another writer; you can guide, follow, or meet head on. How you navigate depends on your wants, needs, and desires. Do you feel like leading the songwriting? Or would you rather sit back and see what transpires? What happens if both you and your cowriter want to lead today?

Being aware of how you work best, how much you are willing to bend, and how much you want to be challenged is your ticket to a cowrite you feel confident about and can learn and grow from.

Part of my purpose in writing this book is to help you know yourself better and become more conscious of your genuine potential.

Play well with others.

The better you are with relationships, the easier the cowrite will be. Are you agreeable or difficult? Are you flexible or unchangeable?

Remember that you are part of a team the moment you involve someone else in the songwriting process. Team-building results in self-development, positive communication, leadership skills, and the ability to work closely together to solve problems.

One evening, while I was guiding cowrites in my weekly workshop, I noticed one participant was badgering her cowriter rather than clearly expressing what she wanted. Not surprisingly, her partner got defensive and shut down communication. He was reacting negatively to her tone of voice and behavior. If she had simply expressed herself more clearly and directly, her cowriter would have most likely been more open to her suggestions. She did not realize that she needed to ask him to come to the workshop prepared with musical ideas so that she could focus on the lyrics, and the cowrite was suffering as a result of this.

The way we use our words and how we communicate can make or break a cowriting relationship—and ultimately the end product.

Protect yourself.

When you cowrite, you agree to create a product together, which can result in a music placement of some type (cover, cut, license, etc.) that has the potential to pay royalties. Before you leave the room, it is important that you and your cowriter have an agreement in place about song splits (who owns what percentage of the song). At the end of this section, you will find a form to assist you in this process.

Pay attention to the chemistry.

Cowriting songs is like co-owning a startup company. You are partnering with another individual to create a product that combines both of your perspectives and experiences. The right combination creates magic.

Pick cowriters who complement your skill set, are pleasant to be around, have good character, and have synergy with you. Good chemistry is so important.

True story: I heard Keith Urban for the first time when he performed at the Academy of Country Music Awards show in 2001. His voice was rich, his songwriting was clever, and when he played that guitar of his— well, there were just no words.

I had just signed songwriter John Shanks, who was coming off producing the Michelle Branch album *The Spirit Room*, and was guiding him to integrate more country into his repertoire. From the get go, I knew that John and Keith would be great together. They were both talented guitarists who would inevitably bond over their shared respect for their instruments.

I called Keith's manager to pitch John as a possible cowrite and before I knew it, they had spent their first day together. Keith walked in with an opening riff, and the rest is history.

Their hit song "Somebody Like You" spent six weeks at the top of the Billboard charts. In December 2009, Billboard named it the number one country song of the first decade of the 21st century. It was John's first and Keith's second number one hit. Now, that was a successful cowrite.

Judy's Must-Read: Victor Wooten's book *The Music Lesson* is an absolute must read.

Use a cowriter initiation form.

Each time you finish a writing session, fill out this form with your partner in the room. That way, you can establish right then and there on paper who wrote what and what the splits will be. Nothing is worse than putting this process off and having trouble remembering the details later on. I have included a template here that you can copy. I recommend keeping a dozen forms printed out to have at your fingertips. It shouldn't be awkward to talk about splits—it's just good business!

The form on the following page will come in handy when you start cowriting.

Co-Writer Information Form

Song Title: _____ **Completion Date:** _____

	Writer 1	Writer 2	Writer 3	Writer 4
Name				
Email				
Publishing				
PRO				
Split				

Available to cut: _____ **On Hold:** _____

Notes:

Signatures:

5

MANUFACTURING YOUR PRODUCT
From Concept to Reality

Art is making something out of nothing and
selling it.

— Frank Zappa

Now, here's the fun part! This is where you get to take your songs from page to product.

No matter what kind of product you make, you will need to make a demo of the song in order to sell it. No one is exempt from this step: a music publisher will expect that you can either make demos yourself, or that you have a team in place to do it.

I advise my clients that, at the very least, they should be able to record their music on the piano or guitar accompanied by their voice.

If you are also interested in producing your own songs, you will need to figure out how to make a quality demo in a limited amount of time. The process of demoing pushes many writers off course. It takes approximately four hours for a simple one instrument (piano/guitar) and voice demo, ten hours for a demo including other instrumentation, and twenty hours or more for a really great demo. Given these timelines, one of the challenges for a songwriter who is not technically gifted is finding a way to get their demos recorded.

It's easy to find a producer who can make a $1,000 demo. When you are starting out, however, and need to demo a lot of songs so that you can learn about the process of writing and recording, this kind of financial commitment can be daunting.

If you are at the beginning and need a simple solution, go to your local music stores, colleges, music organizations, and clubs and seek out an up-and-coming producer who is looking for an opportunity to hone their craft. Not only will this afford you the chance to create your product on a budget, but you will gain the valuable experience of learning how to guide someone else to get what you need.

This is also a wonderful opportunity to practice your leadership skills, which we will discuss in *Chapter 8*.

The more capable you are of guiding (or being) a producer, the more valuable you will be to a music publisher. How you hear your song is one thing: how you communicate your vision to the producer is another. Combining both skills is how you will arrive at a successful demo.

True story: In 2011, Jordan Higgins became the first participant in my mentorship program. He did a little of everything around the office but, more importantly, he produced songs for my catalogue and community of writers.

The next year, I signed Big Machine recording artist RaeLynn after seeing her perform in a singing competition. She had only written one song at the time (it was cowritten with her cousin), and she had no studio experience.

I recognized her potential and had Jordan lead her through the process of putting the first recording together for her song "Baby That's My Type". She learned how to play the guitar to a metronome, record multiple takes of her voice, and combine different segments of her performance to make a demo. I took RaeLynn's demo to Nashville a few weeks later to play it for record executives. That one song began her career path and started her off on building her catalogue, collecting cowriters, and demoing her songs.

Judy's Must-Read: *Modern Recording Techniques* by David Miles Huber and Robert E. Runstein is a great resource for your new demoing adventures.

Here's a list of the seven basic recording essentials you'll need to manufacture your product.

1. Computer with an audio interface.

An audio interface connects your microphone, instruments, and studio monitor to your computer. This converts the sound you hear (the audio) into digital information, which is recorded to your computer, and also converts this digital information back into audio so you can play back what you've recorded.

2. USB condenser microphone.

Typically, when it comes to microphones, the condenser is the most universal in terms of recording applications. This type of microphone is fantastic for vocals, acoustic guitars, and piano. The benefit of using a USB condenser microphone is that it acts as both the microphone and the audio interface.

3. Digital audio workstation (DAW).

This is the software you use to record, edit, and mix records (GarageBand, Pro Tools, Logic Pro, Acoustica Mixcraft, FL Studio, and Audacity are a few examples).

4. MIDI keyboard.

A MIDI keyboard is used to write MIDI (Musical Instrument Digital Interface) information into the DAW, which allows musical instruments to communicate with each other and with your computer.

5. Headphones.

It's so important to invest in a good pair. You will need headphones to listen to what's being recorded as you record it, as well as for referencing your mix later on. Closed-back headphones are recommended.

6. Studio monitors (speakers).

Invest in a good set. Find speakers specifically designed for "reference monitoring" in a recording environment. The purpose of these monitors is to give you a true representation of what is going on within your song while mixing, so you can make accurate adjustments as you work.

7. Miscellaneous – XLR cable, pop filter, and microphone stand.

The XLR cable connects the microphone to the interface. The pop filter prevents "plosives" (the bursts of air that come from hard "B" and "P" sounds) from being picked up by the microphone. The microphone stand will help prevent any noise from being picked up from handheld movement. It's also an essential tool if your hands are busy playing an instrument while you sing.

You may also want to look into a start-up package that combines everything you need for one all-inclusive price. Contact a local or online music shop for advice on which specific products are best for you.

6

AN ARMY OF ONE
Protecting Yourself and Your Songs

*If you don't drive your business, you will be driven
out of business.*

— B.C. Forbes

There are two important steps to take to ensure that you
get paid and get credit for your songs.

Copyright your songs.

Upon completing the recording process for your song, you
have created something and thus own the copyright to it.
You are the owner of this product for the life of the
copyright, beginning on the date that the product (your
song) was created. When you copyright a song, you are
enabling yourself to prove the date of its creation by
registering it in your country's copyright office. In the US,

you would send the song to the Library of Congress, and in Europe, to the European Copyright Registration Service. Contact your local government office for further details on copyright in your area, or perform an online search for more information.

The first step is to make a physical product to send to the copyright office. This physical product can be in the form of a CD, sheet music, video, or USB drive. The next step is to register your work with the Library of Congress at www.copyright.gov, the EU Copyright Office at www.songrite.eu, or the relevant government body in the country where you live. This process should not be overly complicated, and the peace of mind you will gain from knowing that your song is legally protected is reason enough to take the time to do it.

Please note that titles, chord progressions, and overall concepts cannot be copyrighted. Melodies and lyrics, however, can be.

Join a Performing Rights Organization (PRO).

When you get a song played publicly, whether it be on terrestrial (land-based) radio, Internet radio, licensed to a TV show, or played at a club, you are going to need someone to collect your performance royalties. Performance royalties are the revenues due to the songwriter and music publisher when a song is publicly broadcast.

A Performing Rights Organization, or PRO, is the company that collects payments from radio stations and other venues each time your song is played publicly.

In the United States, there are three major PROs: ASCAP, BMI, and SESAC. However, because of our ever-growing digital world, new options are being explored in terms of the ways that royalties are collected. Each PRO approaches their business a little differently, although they all work fundamentally in the same way. The biggest differences are that ASCAP is member-run, while BMI is run by broadcasters and SESAC is invite-only.

When deciding which PRO is right for you, the best thing to do is to educate yourself on each organization and weigh the facts to determine which one will serve you the best.

Here are some things to consider when making your decision:
— Read up on how each PRO was formed
— Learn about their payment schedules
— Understand the terms of their respective contracts
— Meet the reps you would be communicating with and some of the people who make up the community of each society

You may be wondering when would be the right time to join a PRO. It's all up to you: you can wait until one of your songs has been released and royalties are being generated, or you can join beforehand in preparation of releasing your first song. A big benefit of joining sooner rather than later is that you will be able to take advantage of the community that the PRO of your choice has to offer. There are grants, workshops, meet-ups, and networking events all at your disposal.

True story: In 2006, I co-led the Lester Sill Workshop with ASCAP'S Brendan Okrent. The workshop, named after ASCAP's late board member and industry pioneer Lester Sill, focuses on the discovery, development, and education of a select group of sixteen songwriters. We spent two days per week for a whole month providing these songwriters with as much information about the world of songwriting as possible, while igniting their creative inspiration at the same time. They got to do everything from cowriting to learning what a music supervisor looks for in a song for film and TV placements.

After the workshop ended, I signed workshop participant David Choi to his first publishing deal. I worked with Gabriel Mann, who cowrites with my clients, and rooted for Reeve Carney playing the lead in Broadway's Spiderman, as well as Leland Grant when he made it to the battle rounds on The Voice's second season.

That workshop paved the way to a lot of those writers' careers, and the bonds they forged out of that experience has supported them in a business where connection is key amongst so much competition.

Get into the habit of taking care of business for each and every song you write. Your future self will be grateful that you did when, in ten years from now, a TV show wants to use a song you wrote and you have the music, lyrics, cowriter information, and copyright paperwork all ready to go!

Judy's Must-Read: *Songs That Changed Our Lives* by Bruce Birch shows us that you never know how your story will affect someone else.

Here is some further information on the leading PROs:

ASCAP (The American Society of Composers, Authors and Publishers)

– Created and controlled in 1914 by composers, writers, and music publishers
– The board of directors is elected by its membership of 500,000
– They are located in New York, Los Angeles, Nashville, Atlanta, London, Miami, and Puerto Rico
– Members include Justin Timberlake, Diane Warren, Duke Ellington, Dave Matthews, George Gershwin, Stevie Wonder, Beyoncé, Marc Anthony, and Henry Mancini

BMI (Broadcast Music, Inc.)

– Founded in 1939 by radio executives as a non-profit
– They now boast more than 600,000 members
– The company has locations in New York, Los Angeles, Nashville, London, Atlanta, Miami, and Puerto Rico
– Members include Mariah Carey, Lady Gaga, Taylor Swift, Eminem, Rihanna, Maroon 5, Sam Cooke, Willie Nelson, and Dolly Parton

SESAC (Society of European Stage Authors and Composers)

– Note that this abbreviation is meaningless in practice today, as their vision and geographical scope have broadened.

– Founded in 1930, SESAC is the only PRO in the US that is not open to all songwriters; instead, you must receive an invitation to join

– It is also the smallest PRO in the US, with about 30,000 members

– They have locations in New York, Los Angeles, Nashville, Atlanta, Miami, and London

– Members include Bob Dylan, Neil Diamond, Cassandra Wilson, Zac Brown, and Mumford & Sons

During your initial PRO meeting, don't forget to inquire about the following:

What are their fees?

_____

_____

_____

_____

How do they pay out?

_____

_____

_____

How long do contracts with them typically last?

_____

_____

_____

_____

_____

Did you connect with a representative that you believe will have your best interests in mind?

_____

_____

_____

_____

_____

_____

Ask fellow writers about their experience, while trusting your own instincts.

7

SET YOUR MIND TO IT
Self-Motivation

*People often say that motivation doesn't last. Well,
neither does bathing — that's why we recommend it
daily.*

— Zig Ziglar

Did you know that self-motivation is a mindset? You have
a choice, even when you don't think you do. You can take
matters into your owns hands and make a plan.

How do you create a new mindset? Having a
positive attitude that will support you on your journey is
key. It will get hard along the way, and it's especially in
those difficult times that you should be able to give
yourself a pep talk, looking at yourself in the mirror and
telling yourself, "You can do this!"

Like the example from *Chapter 1* of doing
handstands even when you don't think you can, you need

to find ways to gain the confidence to really know that you can achieve your goals. Self-motivation is what drives you to accomplish your goals. It is the essential tool for realizing your dreams.

Here are two basic methods of self-motivation that I personally have found to be effective.

Intrinsic – The internal desire to engage in an activity or perform a behavior for no reason other than the pure enjoyment of developing a skill or learning new material.

Extrinsic – External factors that prompt you to engage in an activity or perform a behavior in order to earn a reward or avoid a punishment.

Ask yourself: What is your true intention? Are you generally more motivated by praise from others, or do you do something because it is personally rewarding? Do you play a sport because you love the sport itself, or because you might win an award? Maybe the answer is a bit of both, but it's important to be aware of what drives you.

Now let's take a look at how you motivate yourself:

Start small.

Don't overwhelm yourself with too much, too soon. Start with setting up one cowriting session a week, not five!

Track your progress.

This will imbue you with the sense of purpose you need to keep going. It shows you the positive outcomes of your hard work, and that can drive you closer to your goals.

Be kind to yourself.

During this process, it is very important that you remember to take breaks. Go for a long walk, forgive yourself for making mistakes, and reward yourself when you complete an important task. For example, when I finish this book, I am treating myself to a long massage!

Challenge yourself.

Make a bet with yourself and keep it!

Keep learning.

Getting restless? It may be a great time to enroll in a class that will spark new ideas.

Surround yourself with support.

Keep people around you who are going to encourage and support your vision.

Ask yourself one last question: are you hungry to be a great songwriter? The answer has to be a loud and joyful "YES", because you have to want to be a songwriter more than anybody else does. Your need to succeed will have to be greater than your fear of failing.

True story: Katy Perry fully embodies the ethos of self-motivation. The majority of my time with her was spent during the period of uncertainty that came between the end of her first record deal and her blow-up debut. During this interval, she was taking some much-needed time to focus on self-development.

Katy had spent years trying to please record executives with her music so that it would get released. But no matter what she did, they always sent her back to the drawing board to do it again.

I resonated with Katy when she lamented not being heard by those who were supposed to be helping to lead her career. I knew that my responsibility to her extended to not only sharing my knowledge and experience of the music business, but also to imparting how she as an individual could gain her own power.

Whenever I would guide her, be it on a small issue or a serious problem, she listened with surround sound, integrated my suggestions into her life, and benefited from the imparted knowledge in some way. Each time, she took a step closer to being a little happier and more secure about where she was going and how she was going to get there. And believe me, it didn't take long, because when she finally stopped and listened to herself, she found that she knew exactly what she wanted!

Katy wants her life and career to happen on her own terms, and in her heart, she knows that she is the only person who can make that happen. She has found her personal power in her self-love, by first giving herself what she needs, knowing that only when she is happy and fulfilled can she give of herself to those around her.

Katy now has millions of people who share in her vision that she has created. They uphold it for her every day, making it easier in the long run for her to achieve the life she always dreamed of.

Judy's Must- Read: *The Four Agreements* by don Miguel Ruiz gives you great principles to practice in your life.

To self-motivate, ask yourself what you want and how you're going to get it.

1. Add structure to your day.

Having a set routine is a recipe for productivity. This is what works for me. I have taken the decision-making into my own hands, and I choose to wake up at the same time each morning (6:30 am). This allows me to know what to expect, and so I can plan my day accordingly, saving me time in the long run.

2. Instill discipline.

Start every day with a mantra, some time for meditation, or a simple walk. It is through the consistency of your actions and your routine that you will see results. I like to start my day with the following prayer from Ho'oponopono, an ancient healing practice of forgiveness from Hawaii practiced throughout Polynesian cultures:

I'm sorry, forgive me, thank you, I love you.

What are three things that you can commit to? Some examples could be a daily walk, practicing yoga once a week, or regular vocal toning in the car on your way to work or school.

3. Gain flexibility.

You don't have to do things the way they've always been done. Your imagination is your consciousness with intent! At one time, giving away a single download of a song for free was unheard of, until one promotion executive had the idea to give fans a token of thanks (and, more importantly, to use this as a way to promote the artist's latest album). Breaking rules and being in more than one project paved the way for Joy Williams to go from being a solo artist to part of The Civil Wars, and then back to a solo career!

Come up with three innovative ideas of your own, then go for it as if no one is looking and no one is holding you back. Use your intention to fuel your imagination. That's when the magic happens.

4. Be committed.

Remember why you are doing this in the first place. Write your intentions down in a journal and revisit it often to keep your focus. Have fun! Reward yourself from time to time, and don't forget to enjoy the creative process.

8

YOU ARE THE CEO
Become the Leader of Your Career

*A leader is best when people barely know he exists,
when his work is done, his aim fulfilled, they will
say: we did it ourselves.*

— Lao Tzu

When I meet a songwriter who is serious about building
their career, I tell them right from the start that they have
to treat it like a business if it's going to work.

You have started your own company creating
songs, which makes you the CEO. Your work ethic and
ability to communicate with others about your business is
vital, as is your ability to manage your creative and
personal life. It is always very important to me that my
clients take care of their business. I guide them to be
organized in registering their songs, wise about who they
hire for their team, and educated about the contracts they

sign. How you interact and conduct yourself with everyone from your team to your cowriters and music executives will be a big deciding factor when it comes to whether or not they will want to work with you.

Here are three steps you can put in place to become the CEO of your company.

1. Create a vision and a mission statement for your company.

A vision statement is the reason why you get up every day and do what you do. A mission statement is how you plan to get there. Having both in place will help you set and reach your goals.

2. Surround yourself with a great team of experts who can help guide you in all areas of business, including the creative and personal aspects.

If you can't afford your "dream team" at first, supplement it with family and friends. Leverage your connections. Maybe you have a family friend who is a lawyer, a significant other well versed in social media, or a sibling willing to sell merchandise at your shows.

One of the benefits I had while working within corporate America was having a team of professionals at my disposal to help me do my job. When I was at Warner Chappell Music, I had a legal team, a film and TV department, IT services, a royalties department, production facilities, and a marketing team at my fingertips at all times.

But when I started my own company, I had only myself to rely on. That all changed once I began building my own team, starting with one part-time assistant, then adding an intern, and finally forming a full-service team made up of interns, a mentorship program, part-timers, and consultants who are all, I might add, budding songwriters. I am proud of this talented group of amazing people that have been with me as I built my business from the ground up, giving me support in structuring my company. In turn, I am able to guide and develop the talents of the people on my team.

3. Become a leader.

Decide what the word "leader" means to you, and then live and lead by example. My definition of a good leader is someone who says to their team, "How do I help you do your job better?"

Throughout the years, I have worked with great leaders; however, I certainly had a few who did not share their visions effectively with the rest of the team, and it became increasingly difficult to follow them as a leader, since we had no idea where they were going!

Now, as the leader of my own company, I have a team in place that adheres to my vision and mission statement, and we all have a clear picture of where we are going. I hold weekly meetings with my staff, allowing the time and space necessary to exchange the ideas and information that will help us all to form a unified front and do each of our jobs better.

I also am very aware that my leading style can differ depending on whether I am working one-on-one with a writer or guiding a big group.

My whole career has been focused on leading songwriters in their careers, and one way I do this is by challenging them to push beyond their comfort zones.

In the late 1990's I produced a writers camp seven years in a row, taking twelve of our writers, from all over the world and with various musical backgrounds, away for a week to write under different circumstances and with different cowriters. I purposely looked for ways to take them away from their everyday routines.

With the help of one head of production, one assistant, and a studio engineer, I chose five houses grouped close together in Lake Arrowhead, organized travel, stocked all of the houses with food, and prepared nightly dinners at the house where I was staying, which we dubbed "the Grand Hall".

Each day, I combined three different writers who then had the day to write and create a simple demo of a song. I would go from house to house, critiquing and guiding them along the way.

At dinnertime, I would put questions to the group to encourage discussion; one night, for example, I would ask them which performing rights society they preferred (see *Chapter 6*), and you should have seen the room light up when they gave their responses! After dinner, they would all sit around the fire and sing and tell stories to each other, which was always my favorite part.

This experience allowed each songwriter to use their skill sets to forge new relationships, process new information, and create something new under a defined time limit. Following this process allowed me the time and space to witness how the songwriters under my guidance handled these new tools, so that I could then guide them to develop even further.

The concept of doing something you don't usually do, or something you are afraid of doing, pushes you through the threshold created by the tension of "doing or not doing". That doorway is what leads to your development, and as I personally can vouch, sometimes we all need a little push to get through that doorway to go where we need to go. When I lead, I always make sure that the person I am guiding knows that it is worth it.

A few more suggestions on becoming an effective leader:

Get experience in leading.

It's as easy as starting a book club. You can invite the participants, decide the agenda, make the first book selection, and host the first meeting to become a role model for other book clubs. In what areas of your life can you become a leader?

Gain exceptional knowledge of the music industry.

Read trade magazines, take classes, and mingle with your peers.

Become a good communicator.

Get in the habit of scripting your requests or responses before you email or meet in person.

Garner respect.

By keeping your word, you will show your integrity to those you interact with.

True story: I worked closely with songwriter, producer, and musician Jamie Houston for over nine years. I met him in Nashville right before he moved to LA in 1992. He had been waiting tables, writing songs, and making connections, and had decided to move to LA to pursue songwriting. A year later, I signed him to his first publishing deal.

From the beginning, I could tell that Jamie was a very quick learner who was inherently good at business and also really great at predicting the future. When he started to earn money from songwriting, he treated every cut as if it could be his last, saving and investing wisely. On my suggestion, he hired a business manager immediately to make sure that, from the very start, he was pointing himself in the right direction.

The music business can be so up and down: you can make $1 on one song and $1,000,000 on the next, so saving up for a rainy day is key.

Jamie brings consciousness to his business practices so that he is protected and isn't caught off-guard when things don't work out. He asks the right questions so that he understands the choices he needs to make.

He also carries all of these skill sets over when he is developing artists, teaching them not only about the creative side but making sure they understand the business. He is paying it forward!

When it came time to hire a lawyer, a business

accountant, and a manager, Jamie hired wisely and has the same team in place to this day. I have watched him balance his career and personal life as he has grown from a young man with aspirations to be a part of the music business, to a successful songwriter, husband, and father. Jamie is a great leader by the example he sets in his creative, business, and personal life.

Judy's Must-Read: Study Robert Greene's *The 48 Laws of Power* to learn how people tend to think.

Here are three important steps you can take when starting your own company:

1. Create a vision board.

Making a vision board is a method of organizing your goals. There are many options on how to construct one. You can find and post pictures on Pinterest, paste pictures on a large poster board, or take all of your pictures and put them in a scrapbook or beautiful box.

The point is to have them be accessible so that you can see them easily and be inspired by the images you have chosen to represent your future.

Here is what you will need to create a poster board version:
– Pictures cut out of magazines or printed from the Internet of people, places, or things that inspire you on your path to be a successful songwriter

– Glue or tape
– Scissors
– Poster board

Arrange the images on your vision board to represent what you want out of your career. Add in any quotes or affirmations that inspire you. Ask yourself what you see yourself achieving in the next year. How about the next five, ten, or twenty?

Step back and take a good look at your vision board. Write down the main theme that jumps out at you. Be specific: is it career, love, family, or something entirely different? Display your vision board in a place where you will see it every single day.

I have been making vision boards for years, and find it so helpful to be surrounded by images of what I want to create. Sometimes I forget that they are photos from a magazine and not from my own life!

2. Write a vision statement and a mission statement.

Your vision statement is the rudder on your ship. It will keep you focused on your goal. When making any and all decisions, you should ask yourself, "Does this support my vision?"

Here is The Judy Stakee Company's vision statement:

> *To illuminate the consciousness of humanity by inspiring, nurturing and protecting the creative process.*

Your mission statement clarifies how you intend to bring your vision to fruition. The Judy Stakee Company's mission statement is as follows:

> *To empower artisans of the music industry to find their own voice and language by challenging them to evolve, thus co-creating a community that fosters integrity, wisdom, and extraordinary moments.*

3. Write your own bio.

This is one of the most helpful tools you can implement when starting your own company. You are defining your "character" as it will be presented to the outside world, and will gain clarity about how you're presenting yourself by creating a script that will introduce you to people in the industry. You will be able to put it in your presentation package introducing you along with your songs, and you can also put it up as a page on your website introducing yourself to the public.

Write from the perspective of your personal brand and your unique take on life. Consider these tips when drafting your bio:

– Ask yourself: who will be reading it?
– Keep it short and simple
– Write in the third person
– List your education and relevant experience
– Name your accomplishments
– Provide your contact info

9

MONEY MAKES THE WORLD GO 'ROUND
Generating Royalties

Money won't create success, the freedom to make it will.

— Nelson Mandela

Royalties are the income that your songs will generate when they are cut and released by you or another artist, licensed for film or TV, played on the radio, performed live, or printed in the form of sheet music.

Record Royalties (Physical and Digital)

Mechanical – You will receive a set royalty rate when your song is reproduced onto CD, DVD, record, or tape (any physically tangible medium).

Performance – You will receive a set royalty rate each time your song is publicly performed (any medium that can be heard).

Film and TV Royalties (commercials, digital media, or any visual paired with sound)

Master Sync – A fee paid for the actual studio recording.

Composition Sync – A fee paid for the use of a song.

One of the great advantages of having a publishing deal is that you have the potential to receive an advance against your future royalties. One of the purposes of this advance is to enable you to be financially stable, so that you have the freedom to put one hundred percent of your time into developing yourself and building your career.

A songwriter's objective is to recoup and exceed the advanced amount in royalties, so that you can continue to generate income on the backend. If your songs are making money before you have even secured a publishing deal, then securing a deal becomes that much easier for you! You have evidence that you are a relatively "safe bet", that any advance a publishing company offers has a better chance of being paid back in full (and then some) since you have money in the pipeline that you can borrow against.

Royalties are collateral (not that different from when you apply for a car or home loan) and validation that your songs have earning potential. For example, if you were to write Kelly Clarkson's next single by yourself, you could likely generate $100,000 from that one track, since she often sells over a million albums and is continuously played on radio. The money would be collected over the following year, but in the meantime, a publisher will feel safe about taking a chance and advancing you $50,000 now. It's really a win-win situation for both parties.

Anything you can do to start generating royalties right away will serve you greatly in the short and long term. This might include getting a cut, releasing an EP, touring and selling merchandise, or getting placements in film and TV. Jump-starting your own career and not waiting around for someone else to do it for you puts you in a much better position!

True story: Tyler Hilton was discovered when he called in to LA radio station KROQ and sang a Johnny Lang cover on the air. The DJs were so impressed that they invited him to their Christmas concert to perform, where a record executive from Warner Brothers saw him and signed him to a record deal. A publishing deal followed, which led Tyler to become one of my writers.

He was 17 years old with a guitar in one hand and a journal in the other, a lot of character in his voice, and so much passion for music. He had been writing a lot of songs by himself, so he started to cowrite and at the same time learned how to demo his own songs.

Tyler was signed to WB for ten years, and although he only released one album and one EP while he was there, the education he received has been invaluable on his journey. During that period, he soaked up all he could about songwriting, producing, touring, and marketing. He was involved in all aspects of his career. For example, he was asked to take a lot of meetings by himself (not always his choice), and through the process he became more and more comfortable as we role-played a fair share of them beforehand. (See *Chapter 10* for more on taking meetings.) At the same time, he was also acting, landing a recurring role on One Tree Hill and playing Elvis Presley in the movie Walk the Line, which provided him with a great platform to release his first record.

Tyler left WB in 2010 and has been the CEO of his own company now for over five years, releasing two albums and continuing his acting career with a recurring role on a new TV series, CBS' *Extant*.

He has gone the independent route, surrounding himself with a great team of professionals who share his vision. And through it all, these experiences have led Tyler to have the kind of life and career he wants, and to be the kind of leader others really want to follow.

Judy's Must-Read: *How to Solve the Mismanagement Crisis* by Ichak Adizes will help you to learn to master decision-making.

The status form on the next page will help you stay organized with all of the details that relate to the production and royalties of your song. Feel free to use this as a template for your projects.

Status Form

Cowriters	%	Lyric	Audio	Artist	Single	LP Title	Label	Release Date	Ownership of the Master

10

HAVE THEM AT HELLO
How to Run a Meeting

When you go to meetings or auditions and you fail
to prepare, prepare to fail. It is simple but true.
— Paula Abdul

If you now have a catalogue of songs, your business in order, and your heart full of intention, then you are ready to start setting up meetings with publishers and other music executives who can help you with the next step: monetizing and expanding your career.

How you present yourself in a meeting and the information you communicate will determine the kind of response you will get. If you are unsure of yourself or your plans and present your vision in a way that is not understandable and enticing, then you're not making the most of your time in the room.

Most importantly, make sure that you respect the time you are being given by being prepared, body, mind and soul (refer back to *Chapter 1* for more on developing these three facets).

Pay attention to how you present yourself, physically, verbally, and socially. Taking a meeting is a face-to-face mode of communication, so what you wear, what you say, and how you behave will all affect the outcome of the meeting.

Also, I want you to know how important a role your voice plays in a meeting. One of my favorite mantras is: "The difference between singing and talking is just a little nuance". The same can be said about the difference between walking and skipping. How you use your voice in a meeting held in an office is just as important as when you are singing a song on stage. Your confidence and excitement will be conveyed through your tone of voice and your choice of words. If you deliver your pitch in a monotone voice for the entire meeting, it will not have the same impact as if you conveyed yourself convincingly through your tone.

If you are inexperienced or unsure of yourself in meetings, try role-playing beforehand. I often run my clients through mock meetings so that they can get comfortable with the process. It's important to learn how to sell yourself in a manner that makes you look both smart and personable.

To improve the meeting experience, most professionals use what is known as "CPR", which in this case stands for context, purpose, and results. It is a method that helps you establish your intention for the outcome of a meeting.

The elements in CPR are put into practice backwards, as follows:

Results: Know what you want.

Purpose: Know why you want these things and how to communicate your desires.

Context: Determine the best words to use to enable you to support your case.

A good friend of mine says that in addition to CPR, he consciously chooses the character he needs to inhabit in order to best communicate his message. Before going into a meeting, he asks himself: "Will I have to be tough and hold my ground even if the other person gets aggressive? Should I be very calm and collected, so that I can read between the lines or bounce jokes back and forth for a few minutes before starting to talk business?" He always says, "I either have to be tough Clint (Eastwood), zen Gandhi, or funny Curly (The Three Stooges)".

When my writers are ready, I take them with me to meetings with record executives, producers, and managers who are actively looking for songs for their artists. This is so that the songwriters can see firsthand what it is like to be in the room while an executive is asking themselves, "Is this song good enough for my artist? Is it good enough to sign you to a deal?" I liken this process to what actors go through on a regular basis in auditions.

For some writers, this can be a nerve-wracking experience, and I have even worked with a few who were dead-set against it. But for the most part, the songwriters I have worked with have loved being that close to the decision-maker, and this experience really helped guide their writing process. They always came away knowing a little bit more about the business.

True story: I worked with songwriter Franne Golde for over fifteen years, and she is a prime example of someone who gives great meetings. She is always personable, funny, smart, and witty, and she really knows her music. These are just a few of the attributes Franne brings to the table in meetings. She also knows how to present the right mix of selling herself and letting the music speak for itself, and the record executives loved her because of these qualities. This allowed her to have a closer relationship with them, which in turn led to her being able to jump on projects early, get the inside scoop, or get a song in at the last minute.

On a Friday night she will never forget, Franne fought bumper-to-bumper traffic to hand deliver a song she had just finished cowriting with Kasia Livingston and Robert Palmer called "Stickwitu" to then-A&M President and producer Ron Fair and producer Tal Herzberg. Despite the fact that Franne had been told the Pussycat Dolls' record was already complete, she refused to take no for an answer. Ten minutes after leaving the studio, Ron called her back and said he had good news and bad news: while the Pussycat Dolls' album was already done, he loved her song and was going to play it for Mary J. Blige on the following Monday. Later that same day, another phone call from Ron came: Mary didn't think the song was right for her, but both Ron and Jimmy Iovine (then-Chairman of

Universal Music) loved it and thought it had the potential to be a smash hit. Despite the fact that the Pussycat Dolls' album was complete, they were going to have them cut the song anyway. This proves an old saying in the music business: "Nothing's final till it's vinyl!"

Countless demos are sent to producers and record executives every day by songwriters hoping to get cuts. Many remain untouched. But Ron knew that if Franne Golde took the time to hand deliver her latest song to him, it would be a gem that could potentially add to the project he was creating. He knew he could count on her, and it had all started with their first meeting.

Judy's Must-Read: Derrik Jensen's *Walking on Water* explains the intricacies of writing, teaching and creativity.

Meetings will not only help you to grow relationships within the industry, they will also help you to grow as a songwriter. Not only do I insist that you start taking meetings as soon as possible, I also strongly recommend that you take comprehensive notes before and after each meeting. This will allow you to reflect on the good points and the points that you can improve on for the next meeting.

The next few pages provide a template for you to follow when keeping notes about meetings.

Date: _____ / _____ / _____

Name: _____

Position: _____

Company: _____

Location: _____

_____

Pre-Meeting Questions

What do you know about the person you're meeting with?

_____

_____

_____

_____

_____

_____

What project are you meeting about?

_____

_____

_____

_____

_____

_____

What is your goal? Think about what you hope to gain and what you are bringing to the table.

_____

_____

_____

_____

_____

_____

Post-Meeting Questions

What songs were pitched?

_____

_____

_____

_____

Which artist was pitched?

_____

_____

_____

Was any homework given?

_____

_____

_____

_____

What did you wear? (This is to prevent you from repeating an outfit when meeting with the same person more than once.)

_____

_____

_____

_____

_____

What personal tidbits did you pick up about the person you took the meeting with? Examples include their hobbies, musical taste, and any other relevant personal details.

_____

_____

_____

_____

_____

_____

General notes:

_____

_____

_____

_____

_____

_____

_____

_____

_____

_____

_____

_____

11

A WINNING ATTITUDE WINS

Change Your Story

A winner is someone who recognizes his God given talents, works his tail off to develop them into skills, and uses these skills to accomplish his goals.
— Larry Bird

This is your opportunity to create the life and the career that you want. I don't think that the majority of the population is dialed into the fact that everything in this world was created by people just like them, and that if they want something different, they need to imagine what that would look like and figure out how to make it a reality. Your attitude is what fuels the "figuring out" part.

In my life, there is no "It can't be done": there is only "How can I get it done?" The skill requirements may change depending on the situation, but my attitude is something I choose.

Life can be hard. The music business can be hard, too. Getting songs on the radio or placed on a TV show or in a movie is hard. To quote Tom Hanks in A League of Their Own, "If it was easy, everyone would be doing it!" Get over the "hard" part. Just because it's hard doesn't mean it can't be done.

You can start by changing your story. Did you know that everything in this life is a story? Every book on every shelf is someone's account, their version of what happened. We receive information from all five of our senses and the brain can't help but process it into stories. We use these stories to discover and give meaning to our lives. You can tell yourself that you'll never make it or you can tell yourself that your break is just around the corner. Which one do you think will get you further? Just by rephrasing your words to move your stories in a more forward direction can lead you closer to your goals. Start becoming aware of the intentions you have set for yourself. It starts with your voice.

Tell yourself that you can do it. Rehearse it out loud in front of the mirror if that helps. Say the words over and over and until you start believing them. A good attitude trumps all else.

True story: I am fortunate in my career to have always made sure to work with writers who emanated winning attitudes. They never gave up and they never gave in. Sure, they faced disappointment from time to time, but the fire in their bellies never went out. They all have music running through their veins.

If I had to pick one story that epitomizes this, then it's

Julian Bunetta's. I was first friends with Julian's father, Peter Bunetta, who is an award-winning music producer, so I can safely say the apple didn't fall far from the tree.

Julian came to see me when he was 19 and only writing beats. Although he wasn't writing songs at the time, he really wanted to learn so that he could add that skill to his repertoire. He did, however, know how to produce songs, which gave him an advantage when it came to songwriting. I immediately recognized his potential when I heard how professional his demos were. He instinctively knew how to set the stage for the melody and lyrics. I signed him to a publishing deal and Julian soaked up every word of advice I gave him. He learned how to write a song in no time flat and immediately rewarded us with a cut: "Living with Lonesome" (with Tyler Hayes and Wayne Kirkpatrick) on Little Big Town's debut album, which sold over a million copies.

There have been many times when I have found myself in front of a very talented individual who, unfortunately, had a terrible attitude or an ego that was too big for the room. I walked away each time. Unlike these people, Julian – who had been taught the lesson at an early age that the better you are at what you do, the better the results you will be capable of achieving – knew his attitude was the power of his development. He was a great student.

Julian approaches everything with a smile, creating magic in his life while knowing in his heart that he has the ability to create anything he wants as long as he applies his skills, instincts, and intention. That's a winning attitude.

Judy's Must Watch: *What the Bleep Do We Know?!* Watch for inspiration on being the creative force in your life.

12

WHAT'S NEXT?
Putting It All Together

Say what you wanna say
And let the words fall out
Honestly, I wanna see you be brave
— Sara Bareilles

If you're a confident and consistently good writer with a solid community and network around you, your business is in order, you have the ability to carry yourself well in meetings, and you are respected among your peers, then take a look around: you have started a career for yourself in the music industry.

What are the next steps you should take? You can take a do-it-yourself approach and hire those you need to complete certain jobs. For example, you can hire an independent song plugger, someone who will pitch your songs to projects and take a percentage of any cuts they get for your songs. Or you can sign with a music publisher, and they can take care of all your professional needs for you. Either way, you will have to integrate the lessons you have learned in this book to help your career to grow and thrive!

Use your contacts to start putting together a plan of action. If you go down the do-it-yourself road, what will that look like? Do you have the financial capacity to hire independent consultants? Can you find people who will trade with you or delay commission?

If you decide to explore a music publishing deal, try to meet with more than one music publisher. You will be interviewing them as much as they will be interviewing you, and it will pay to do your research on the company and the executives who will be representing you. Remember how important relationships are. You will be co-creating your career with your music publisher should you choose to go down that road, so look for someone for whom you have mutual trust and respect.

If you've followed the advice in this book, you now have everything going for you in terms of what you need to start building your career, so be intentional in how you put your plan together. Call on your connections, meet with everyone you possibly can, and celebrate what you have accomplished to get to this point!

The process of taking what you have learned and putting it into action is no small task, and that's why I must reiterate the importance of self-motivation and a winning attitude. Right now, put these two essential keys to success in the driver's seat to start the process of taking the next step.

You've got to have the confidence to say to yourself, "I've got this!" and really believe it. That confidence is the spark that will attract fans in the audience as well as in the office. I know this because, as a lifelong music fan myself, I am constantly on the lookout for voices and stories that will spark what's inside of me. That's when I feel most alive and connected. That's the magic. That's the music.

Before you go, I have one more valuable piece of advice to share with you, on the subject of self-love. Self-love is the act of caring, respecting, knowing, and taking responsibility for yourself. Because, when it comes down to it, you are your greatest hope if you want to make it work in the music business, no one else.

Now, this is a concept that is not readily taught and one that I never really practiced myself growing up. I grew up thinking that I was here to please other people first and then myself second, and I know that I have plenty of company in that belief.

One day I finally decided that, with nothing to lose, I was going to start loving myself and see what happened. What does self-love look like? Giving myself what I need and want, first of all. It started with me taking control of my healing process from the stress that had caused my body to start breaking down. I then started respecting what I had to offer in terms of my purpose on this earth, which is to help others to learn how to communicate through songs. The gift of it is that I have found a deep appreciation for my unique body, mind, and soul.

I started feeling so good about myself, and then I noticed that other people in my life were having the same reaction; they were feeling good about me, too! This, in turn, made me feel even more loved. I had come full circle.

I want you to imagine yourself as a glass full of milk, with all your friends and family surrounding you. Visualize the milk being doled out from the glass, nourishing everyone around it, but being depleted in the process. Now visualize yourself as an empty glass, being endlessly replenished with milk. What happens in the second scenario is that the glass (you) overflows, allowing those around you to be nourished without the glass itself being depleted.

Self-love is not selfish; it is empowering. Honor who you are becoming and appreciate the steps you are taking to get there.

I really do know how lucky I was to have gone from college into the music business, where I found happiness and fulfillment for over thirty years. I knew where my place was in the world, and that felt grounding. But when I left the industry in 2009, I found myself asking the same question I did when I first left college: "What now?"

I knew in my heart that I had to leave the business to be able to pursue my own dreams, but walking away was still so painful. As much preparation and planning as I had done, the reality of building a whole new career on my own was daunting. I decided to seek out guidance. The first year after leaving the business, I hired one of the top business, personal, and creative consultants to help me build my business. At the same time, I dove into being creative myself: writing songs, taking acting classes, musical theater workshops, voice over and comedy classes. When it came down to it, each class I took dealt with the voice, lyrics, and melody, but each from a different perspective. When you act, you use your voice, words, and melody: you may not be singing the words, but each scene has its own internal melody. And the difference between singing and taking is really just a little nuance!

I wanted to develop these creative skills for myself, and at the same time I was gaining such great knowledge and ideas for how to develop songwriters from a different perspective. What I noticed was that the more I developed myself, the better teacher I was becoming. I am so grateful for the time, space, and tools I put in place so that I could develop myself from working for someone else to running my own company. It has been an extremely challenging transition to say the least, but one that keeps rewarding me on a daily basis.

True Story: I had been a fan of Wayne Kirkpatrick long before I met him, before he had cowritten with Gordon Kennedy and Tommy Simms on "Change The World", which was recorded by Eric Clapton, produced by Babyface, and used in the end titles to the movie Phenomenon. The song went on to win a Grammy Award in 1997 for Record of the Year, Song of the Year, and Best Male Pop Vocal Performance. Additionally, the song was chosen by the Recording Industry Association of America as one of the Songs of the Century and ranked at number 270.

In 1998, I found out Wayne was at the end of his current publishing deal so I immediately flew to Nashville and, after a three-hour dinner together, would not let him leave the restaurant until he signed with me.

I knew Wayne was the whole package: he has a

beautiful voice, writes lyrics and melodies, is a wonderful guitar player, and has produced and engineered his own songs. The body of work that Wayne created during the near decade we worked together lead to the production of songs for such acts as Little Big Town, Faith Hill, Garth Brooks, Amy Grant, Martina McBride, Wynonna Judd, Trisha Yearwood, and Bonnie Raitt, to name a few!

About five years ago, Wayne decided to spread his wings and create with new materials. He started collecting old games and guitars, turned them into pieces of art, and now has a successful antique business. And with his brother, Karey Kirkpatrick, he has written a musical, "Something Rotten", which has opened to rave reviews on Broadway.

What's next does not have to be a question that rattles you, but instead can get you excited for all the new possibilities that are ahead of you!

Judy's Must-Read: In *Shut Up And Tweet*, Phil Pallen helps you build a better brand.

Last Thoughts

It has been a privilege to tell you my story. The vision for
this book started out as a short "how to" that has now
turned into a dialogue, one that's just getting started. And
I could not be happier to finally be here with you.

As you continue along your journey, integrating
everything you have learned in this book, you will be faced
with the challenge of breaking down old patterns and
behaviors, and replacing them with new ideas and
perspectives. Those old patterns are like walls that are
there to protect you, although in the process they have
become limiting to you. It's important to know that you
don't necessarily have to tear these walls down; instead,
you can build windows and doors in them, opening

yourself up to new ideas. If you are aware that you have a choice, you can widen your perspective.

So go ahead and imagine yourself sitting in a comfortable, spacious room (like the one we talked about in *Chapter 2*), the walls painted white and just waiting for you to decorate them. There's a piano and a guitar in one corner, a yoga mat on the floor, and a journal at your side filled with your favorite quotes. The room houses a small studio to record your demos and stacks of books for you to reference while songwriting (including this one!). It's all there waiting for you.

This book is like my song, a song that expresses my unique perspective and draws on all my years of experience. Through the lessons outlined in these pages, I have used my voice, melody, and lyrics to tell a story that will hopefully inspire you to go and tell your own story. It's one the world needs to hear.

Judy's Must-Read: *The Pilgrimage* by Paulo Coelho is an inspiring journey of the self.

Final Checklist

□ Songs are your calling card. Always.

□ Creativity and the ability to take risks are requirements for success.

□ Everything we are about in this life is in relation to someone or something else.

□ Make sure that the company you choose to work with conducts their business to your standard and represents you in the best light.

□ When you're cowriting, be intentional, play well with others, protect yourself, and pay close attention to the chemistry.

▫ You'll need to make a model or demo of your song in order to sell it. At the very least, you should be able to record a piano or guitar vocal on your own. Self motivation is the essential tool for pursuing your goals.

▫ Challenge yourself. Be willing to take risks and make mistakes. Don't quit. Choose joy and dare to dream big!

▫ A creative process is a series of actions, changes, and functions that are put in place to bring about a result.

▫ Think about what time, space, and tools you need in order to develop and produce yourself and your songs.

▫ Take responsibility for your own learning and development.

▫ You are the CEO of your company.

▫ Surround yourself with a great team of experts who can help guide you in all areas of business, both creative and personal.

▫ There are two important steps to take to ensure that you get paid and get credit for your songs: copyright your songs and join a PRO.

□ Anything you can do to start generating royalties right away will serve you greatly.

□ How you present yourself in meetings and the information you communicate are essential to the response you will get.

□ Pay attention to how you present yourself, physically, verbally, and socially.

□ Get over the "hard" part. It can be done.

□ A good attitude trumps all else.

Note from Param Media

The Songwriter's Survival Guide is not only full of very helpful advice for how to become a great songwriter, but it is an inspiring spiritual book as well.

By emphasizing the importance of developing the body, mind, and soul, this book is a wonderful example of how a deeper understanding of one's self can lead to a much more meaningful life in general, in addition to achieving a successful career in the music industry.

Param Media is dedicated to publishing pioneering books, and we hope that Judy's creative vision will continue to have a growing positive impact across the music industry.

Acknowledgements

This book offers you some of the most important advice I have discovered during my many successful years in the music industry. It started out as a small book of what I thought would be no more than twenty pages, but somewhere along the way, my passion got the best of me and it blossomed into a unique creative expression.

From the bottom of my heart, thank you to my team:

Phil Pallen, for the inspiration and polite nudge to write this in the first place.

Andrea Blackie and the editorial team at Param Media, for helping me find my voice through my words.

Lindsay Rush, my chief of staff, for being by my side the whole time, and to Rachel Panchal, Jordan Higgins, and

Justin Muncy for their invaluable input.

Thank you to Lauren Moore and Thanh Nguyen for their expertise in editing and graphics.

I am deeply thankful for the support of my community of friends and family.

A special thanks to Kelly Gitter, my soul sister, for her gift of endless possibilities, and to my husband Brian Murphy, for being the wind beneath my wings.

And to all the songwriters and producers who I have known and worked with, past and present, thank you for giving me the gift of the experiences that allowed this book to come into existence.

Made in the USA
Lexington, KY
10 April 2019